# DEAR,

May the Almighty bless you and your family
with his blessing.

**What is Religion?**
*A guide book for Muslim Kids about Divine Abrahamic Religions*

ISBN: 978-1-990544-95-8

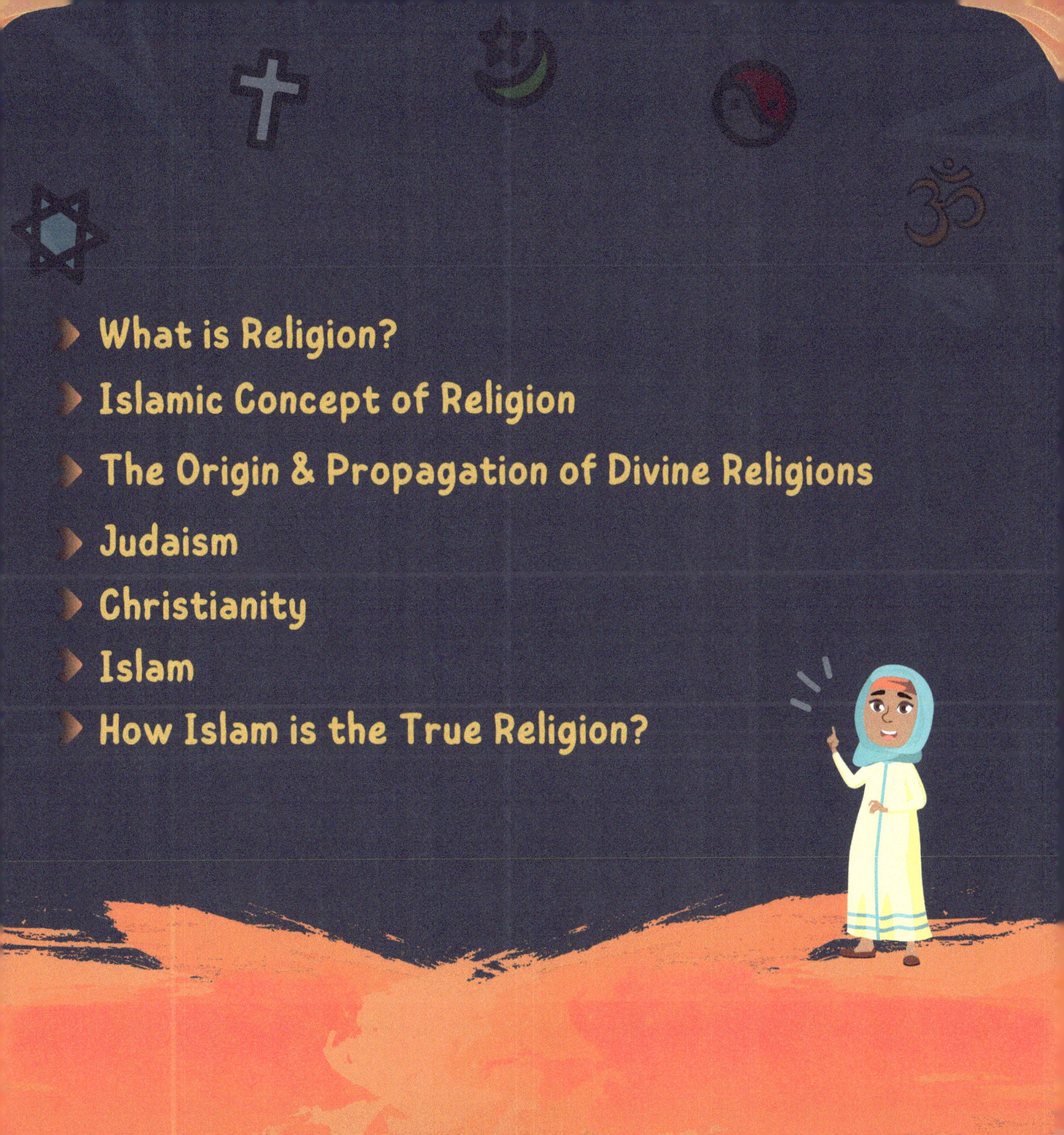

# WHAT IS RELIGION?

According to Encyclopaedia Britannica, Religion is a human beings' relation to that which they regard as holy, sacred, absolute, spiritual, divine, or worthy of especial reverence. It is also commonly regarded as how people deal with ultimate concerns about their lives and their fate after death. Believers and worshippers participate in and are often enjoined to perform religious practices such as prayer or particular rituals. Worship, moral conduct, right belief, and participation in religious institutions are among the constituent elements of the religious life.

From the perspective of religious sciences, some common factors found in all religions can be mentioned as:

• Belief in supernatural creatures (like God, angels, jinn, and spiritual creatures)

• Separation of the sacred and mundane

• Worship, rituals, and ceremonies

• Written or non-written traditions (sacred book, moral code of laws)

• Emotions related to supernatural beings and the sacred (like fear, trust, secrets, sinfulness, worship, devotion)

- Connection to the superhuman (by ways and means like revelation, prophets, prayer, supplication, and inspiration)
- View on this world and man, and life and the afterlife
- Life order
- Social group (community) and belonging to a group

# ISLAMIC CONCEPT OF RELIGION

All branches of knowledge related to religion have defined religion from their own perspective. While describing religion, Muslim Scholars explained the true religion as: "Religion is a divine law that enables people with intelligence to attain goodness and happiness in this world and the next with their own desire."

The word "law" shows us that once we have declared our faith, religion's principles must be implemented in our lives as definite rules and that negligence will be taken into consideration at the divine judgment. Religion to the follower is a living system whose laws should complement the capacity of an individual's daily life and whose results are to be seen in every aspect of life.

According to Islam, only the system sent by Allah(S.W.T) via His Prophets(a.s) is the true religion. In this way, man bowing down to man has been prevented, and it has been established that all people are one and equal before Allah and superiority lies only in the piety of a follower.

In a nutshell, religion is the general name for the divine law, order, and path revealed by Allah(S.W.T) to his Prophets, who then announce and spread the message to the nation, for strengthening the relationship between Allah(S.W.T) and his servants.

# THE ORIGIN & PROPAGATION OF DIVINE RELIGIONS

Islamic faith tells us that the only divine source of all revealed religions is Allah[S.W.T] through His chosen Prophets and Messengers. Each religion manifests a fundamental truth i.e., There is no God but Allah, and He is the only one to be worshipped; but the laws and obligations may be different according to the need and intellectual capacity of the humans of that period, age, or race. The chosen Prophets were always from the community of their residence to help prove their credibility and to ensure the divine guidelines were perceived and performed correctly. All religions came from Allah[S.W.T], and as long as they kept up their perfection, they stayed legitimate. Furthermore, when the time of the demise of a Prophet had come near, he always guides his companions to have faith in Tawhid and wait for the next Prophet.

"O humanity! Indeed, We created you from a male and a female, and made you into peoples and tribes so that you may ˹get to˺ know one another. Surely the most noble of you in the sight of Allah is the most righteous among you. Allah is truly All-Knowing, All-Aware." (Surah Al-Hujurat, 13)

The divine method of Allah(S.W.T) to send his Prophets to a community, is always alligned to their mental capacity and desires. Also, the miracles given to the Prophets is the most powerful attribute among the population to eradicate the sinful practices rooted in them. For instance,

- In the era of Prophet Yusuf(a.s), beauty matters a lot. The beauty of an individual inspired people. Another thing that was of importance is the ability to interpret dreams correctly. So Allah(S.W.T) made Prophet Yusuf(a.s) the most beautiful person as well as gave him the knowledge of interpretation of dreams.

- The nation of Prophet Musa(a.s) excelled at magic, so the staff was one of the miracles given to Prophet Moosa(a.s). By that staff, he defeated the magicians of Pharaoh, extracted water from the rock, and made the way into the sea by the permission of Allah The Almighty so that He would save the believers.

- Allah(S.W.T) gave Prophet Sulaiman(a.s) a massive kingdom, not only in terms of land but also in controlling the jinn, animals, and winds along with human beings.

- Likewise, the people of Prophet Isa(a.s) excelled at medicine, so Prophet Isa(a.s) cured the incurable, the blind and the leper, and gave life to the dead by the permission of Allah The Almighty.

- The Arabs excelled at poetry and rhetoric, and therefore Allah The Almighty revealed Qur'an to Prophet Muhammad ﷺ. It was a miracle that the Arabs were not able to compose even one verse like it. The Holy Prophet ﷺ showed numerous miracles to preach Islam to the Arabs.

This system of Allah(S.W.T) started from the Prophet Adam(a.s) (the first human being on Earth) and ended on the last Prophet, Prophet Muhammad ﷺ, with the religion of Islam, which verifies all the previous Prophets and their religions. In today's world, three major ummah (nations) are present as followers of the religions, whom Prophets are the descendants of Prophet Ibrahim/Abraham(a.s). These Abrahamic Religions are Judaism, Christianity, and Islam, whose followers are called Jews, Christians, and Muslims. Although there are various factions and schools of thought in every religion, their fundamental beliefs are the same.

The Abrahamic Religions are all based on monotheism (belief in One God), and Islam calls them 'The people of the Book' because they all follow a Divine Book as a guide in their religious matters.

# ATHEISM & POLYTHEISM

The other religions and beliefs whose followers are in large number in the modern world are:

- Atheist; The idea of Atheism, i.e., no Divine authority, excepted by Taoism, Buddhism, and Atheism.

- Hindu; Hinduism is the only major religion whose followers believe in polytheism, i.e., worshipping multiple gods.

JUDAISM

# JUDAISM

## ORIGIN

Judaism began in ancient Israel about 4,000 years ago. In this region, Prophet Ibrahim[(a.s)] was the first to declare that there is only one true God. Prophet Musa[(a.s)], centuries later, then led the Jewish people away from slavery in Egypt, which was a defining moment for Judaism.

## BOOK

Prophet Musa[(a.s)] is credited with the revelation of the Torah, the sacred Jewish texts, which consists of the five books of Moses (Prophet Musa[a.s]).

## BELIEFS

Followers of Judaism are monotheistic, believing that there is only one true God. Israel is the sacred land of the Jewish people, and it is seen as a gift to them — the children of Israel — from God. According to the Torah, Jewish believers must live a life of obedience to God; because life itself is a gift granted by God to his disciples (Sanders, 2009). Followers of Judaism live in accordance to the ten commandments revealed to Prophet Musa[(a.s)] by Allah[(S.W.T)] on Mount Sinai. These commandments outline the instructions for how to live life according to God.

# RITUALS AND PRACTICES

Judaism has many rituals and practices that followers of the faith carry out. Jewish people have strict dietary laws that originate in the Torah, called Kosher laws. The goal of these laws is not a concern for health but holiness. Examples of foods that are prohibited include, pig, hare, camel, and ostrich meat, and crustacean and molluscan seafood. Additionally, certain food groups are banned from being consumed when combined, such as meat and dairy (Tieman & Hassan, 2015).

Jewish followers also carry out multiple prayers each day, reaffirming and demonstrating their reciprocal love with God. In the modern world, the majority of Jews are inhabited in the United States and Israel.

# CHRISTIANITY

# CHRISTIANITY

## ORIGIN

Christianity began in approximately 35 CE — i.e., the date of the crucifixion — in the area of the Middle East that is now known as Israel. Christianity began with recognition of the holiness of Prophet Isa/Jesus[a.s]. He was unsatisfied with the alteration of Judaism and took it upon himself to seek a stronger connection to the word of God as defined by the earlier Prophets. Thus, Christianity initially developed as a sect of Judaism. It developed into a distinct religion as Jesus developed a stronger following of those who believed that he was the son of God. The crucifixion of Jesus was the first of many tests of faith of Christians (Guy, 2004). However, according to Islamic belief, Prophet Isa[a.s] was one of the Prophets of Allah, not a son of God. He was not crucified but elevated to the Heavens, only to return near the Day of the Judgment to eliminate all the false beliefs.

A division emerged within Christianity between Eastern Orthodoxy and Roman Catholicism with the Roman Empire's division into East and West. During the Protestant Reformation, a second division occurred when Protestant sects emerged to challenge the Catholic Church and Papacy's authority to be intermediaries between God and Christian believers.

## BELIEFS

At the core, to be Christian is to believe in the trinity of father, son, and holy spirit as one God: The God of love. God allowed his only son to be sacrificed in the crucifixion to compensate for their sins out of love for humanity. Christians are admonished to love God and to love their neighbours and enemies "as themselves." They believe in God's love for all things, have faith that God is watching over them at all times, and that Jesus, the son of God, will return when the world is ready. Jesus is the exemplar of the religion, demonstrating how to be a proper Christian. In the Christian faith, the theodicy, or the way that Christianity explains why God allows bad things to happen to good people, is shown through faith in Jesus. If believers follow in Jesus' footsteps, they will have access to heaven. Unfortunate occurrences are acts of God that test the faith of his followers. Therefore, by maintaining faith in God's love, Christians are able to carry on with their lives when confronted with tragedy, injustice, and suffering.

## BOOK

The Christian Bible is comprised of the Old Testament and the New Testament. The Old Testament dates to hundreds of years before the hour of Christ. The New Testament dates from the hour of Christ, or hundreds of years from that point. The focal books of the Bible for Christians are the Gospels.

# RITUALS AND PRACTICES

There are many rituals and practices that are central to Christianity, known as the sacraments. For example, the sacrament of baptism involves the literal washing of the person with water to represent the cleansing of their sins. Today, the ritual of baptism has become less common; however, historically the process of baptism was considered an integral rite in order to baptize the individual and to wipe away their ancestral or original sin (Hanegraaff, 2009). Other sacraments include the Eucharist (or communion), confirmation, penance, anointing the sick, marriage, and Holy Orders (or ordination). However, not all sects of Christianity follow these.

One of the core qualities and practices of Christianity is caring for the poor and disadvantaged. Jesus, a poor man himself, fed and nurtured the poor, demonstrating care for all, and is thus seen to be the exemplar of morality (Dunn, 2003). Christian churches are often institutions that demonstrate how to follow Jesus, running charities and food banks, and housing the homeless and the sick.

ISLAM

# ISLAM

## ORIGIN

Originating in Arabia, Islam is a monotheistic religion that developed in approximately 600 CE. During this time, the society of Mecca was in turmoil. The birthplace of Prophet Muhammad ﷺ was Makkah. He was from the Banu Hashim Clan of Quraish Tribe and is a descendant of Prophet Ibrahim's [a.s] son, Prophet Ismael [a.s]. Between Prophet Musa [a.s] and Prophet Isa [a.s], all the Prophets are from Bani Israel, i.e., they are the descendants of Prophet Yaqoob [a.s], and there was no Prophet in between Prophet Ismael [a.s] and Prophet Muhammad ﷺ. Prophet Muhammad ﷺ received the verses of the Qur'an directly from the Angel Jibrael a.s during a period of isolated prayer on Mount Hira. After immense struggles and preaching Islam for twenty-three years, he developed a following of people who eventually united Arabia into a single state and faith against polytheistic pagans. Followers of the Islamic faith are referred to as Muslims.

# BOOK

The Qur'an is the central religious text of Islam, believed by Muslims to be a revelation from one God, Allah[S.W.T]. It is widely regarded as the finest work in classical Arabic literature and is organized in 114 Surahs (chapters), consisting of Ayats (verses). Muslims believe that the Qur'an was orally revealed by Allah[S.W.T] to the final Prophet, Prophet Muhammad ﷺ, through the angel Jibrael[a.s], incrementally over a period of 23 years, beginning in the month of Ramadan. Muslims regard the Qur'an as Prophet's most crucial miracle, a proof of his prophethood and the conclusion of a series of divine messages previously revealed to Prophets, including the Tawrah (Torah), the Zabur ("Psalms"), and the Injil ("Gospel/Bible"). The Qur'an describes itself as Al-Kitab (The Book), Al-Furqan (the discernment), Umm al-Kitab (the mother book), Al-Huda (the guide), Al-hikmah (the wisdom), Dhikr (the remembrance), and Tanzil (the revelation; something sent down).

# BELIEFS

The Six Beliefs of Islam are the fundamental beliefs that every Muslim holds to be true.

- Tawhid - Belief in the oneness of Allah
- Malaika - Belief in the existence of angels of Allah
- Belief in the Holy books of Allah; Zabur, Torah, Gospel/Bible, and the Qur'an
- Nubuwwah and Risalah - Belief in All Prophets of Allah, from Prophet Adam (a.s) to Prophet Mohammed ﷺ
- Belief in the day of judgment; a day will come when every human that has ever existed will be judged by Allah about their actions in their life on earth.
- Belief in predestination (destiny/divine decree) - the idea that Allah knows everything

# RITUALS AND PRACTICES

Islam outlines five pillars that must be upheld to become a practical Muslim:

1.  Shahadah; which states that there is no God but Allah, and Prophet Muhammad ﷺ is God's submissive servant and messenger

2.  Salah; Prayer five times daily

3.  Zakah; Providing financial aid to support poor Muslims

4.  Fasting; Participation in the month-long fast during Ramadan, the 9th month of the Islamic calendar

5.  Hajj; Completion of a pilgrimage to Makkah at least once in their life if one can afford

# HOW ISLAM IS THE TRUE RELIGION?

As of now, we have learned that the Abrahamic Religions propagated with time, and numerous Prophets came to deliver the same fundamental message of Tawhid. But the question arises, why it stopped on Islam and why Allah<sup>(S.W.T)</sup> ended this chain of prophethood on the Prophet Muhammad ﷺ.

First of all, we have to understand why the need for new Messengers and Prophets arose when their message was the same? What is the main reason of revealing a new but similar religion?

The single most significant answer to this question is the 'adulteration of the truth' by the nation. From the time of the Prophet's demise till the coming of the next Prophet, the divine truth was eventually corrupted by the people for their worldly gains. Previously, the duty to guard the truth was used to be given to the ummah of the Prophet, but that's not the case for Islam.

Firstly, Allah<sup>(S.W.T)</sup> took the responsibility to protect the originality of the Qur'an till the Day of Judgement. This is the living proof that after more than fourteen-hundred years of its revelation, the Qur'an's text is still the same as before. Secondly, the life of the last Messenger, Prophet Muhammad ﷺ, is a guide for all the humanity to come till the Day of Judgement. The Holy Prophet ﷺ spent the whole life as a common man, but his teachings and decisions are a monument to follow in every dimension of life. As Allah<sup>(S.W.T)</sup> said in Qur'an,

"Indeed, in the Messenger of Allah you have an excellent example for whoever has hope in Allah and the Last Day, and remembers Allah often." (Surah Al-Ahzab, 21)

For a religion to be compatible with the contemporary world, its teachings and laws should be valid and comprehensible by all. Islam shines in every aspect of today's world. Out of all the religions, Islam is the only religion that is subjected to the complete social setup instead of being confined to the subject of religion. The Islamic Sharia' Law, which is based on the teachings of the Qur'an and the traditions of the Prophet Muhammad ﷺ (Hadith and Sunna), is not limited to the religion, rather it also teaches how to establish public relations, political dealings, justice, administration, army, marriage, divorce, peace, war, debt, interest, charity, etc. that are considered to be as necessary as the obligation of the religious rules. Islam is a religion for everyone; it is the most complete manifestation of the truth and provides a straight path and a perfect balance.

After careful comparison of Islam with other religions, we will come to know that the world has also suffered from the one-sidedness of many religions and ideologies. Some have emphasized the material side of life and ignored the spiritual aspects, while others saw the world as an illusion, a deception, and a trap. Islam, however, has a different point of view; It blurs the line between material/worldly desires and moral/spiritual obligations. Islam does not prohibit us from eating delicious food; it refrains us from a limited number of haram foods and allows us to enjoy all the other halal ones. It does not obligate people to remain unmarried to attain a high spiritual status; instead, it is highly desirable in Islam to marry and enjoy family life and other relationships. The core of Islam teaches that the moral and material powers must come together to strengthen faith. Spiritual salvation can be achieved by using material resources for the good of humanity and not by living a life of self-denial or running away from the joys of this world.

Thus, Islam's exceptional characteristics stand out as the religion of humanity, the religion of today, and the religion of tomorrow. Islam is emerging as the fastest-growing religion in the world.

These aspects have won the hearts of hundreds of thousands of people in the past and present and made them affirm that Islam is the religion of truth and the straight path for humankind and will continue to fascinate them in the future. Our sole duty is to study Islam and implement its teachings in our lives as this is the only way to know the truth of this Universe.

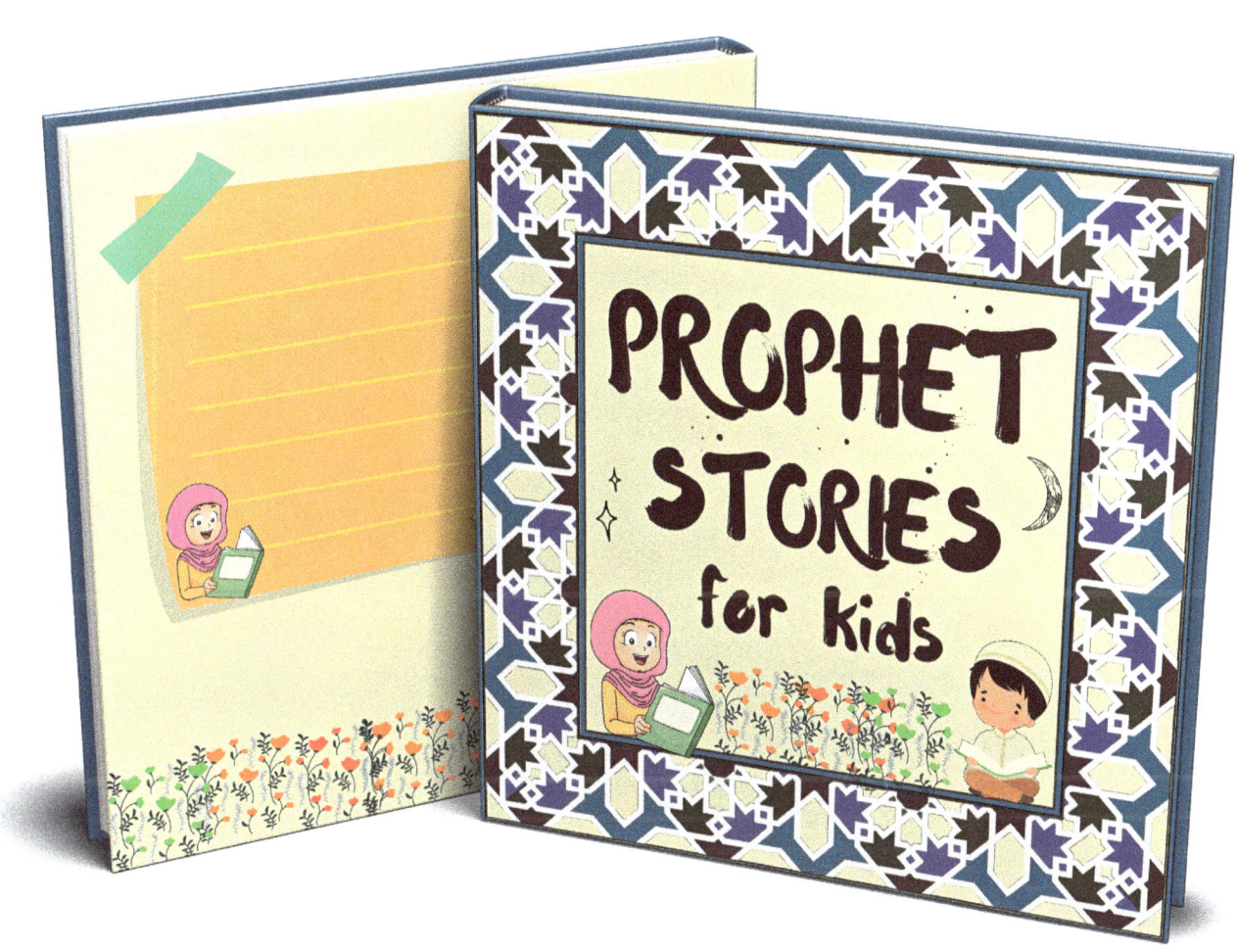

ISBN 978-1-990544-43-9

*Search ISBN on the retailer website

# Premium Color Pages Hardcover

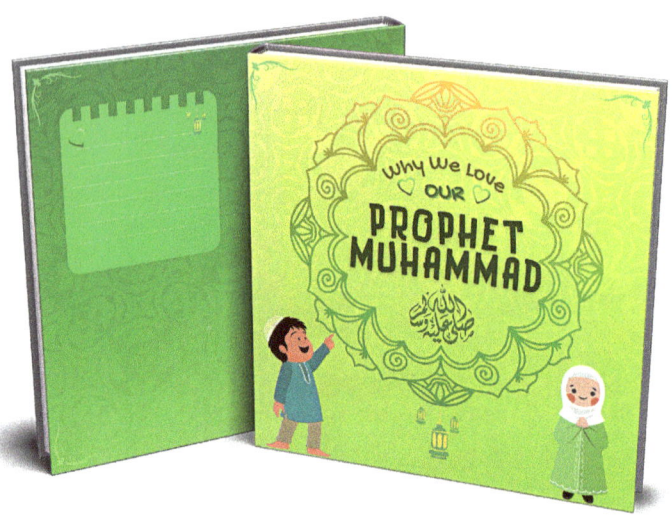

ISBN 978-1-990544-42-2

ISBN 978-1-990544-41-5

ISBN 978-1-990544-45-3

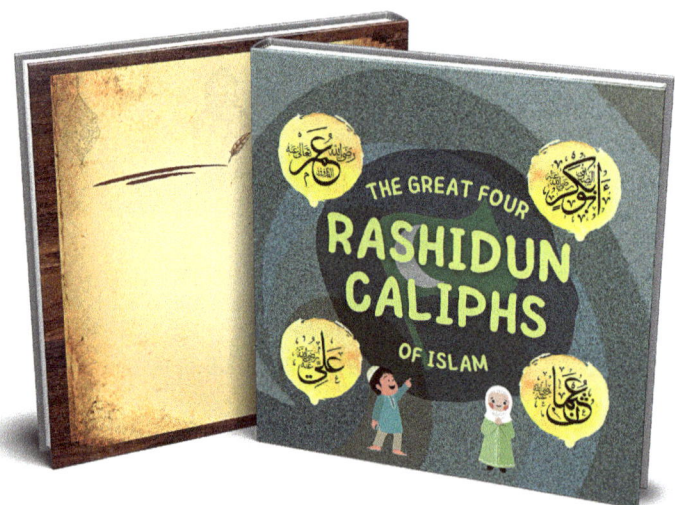

ISBN 978-1-990544-44-6

*Search ISBN on the retailer website